SPACE
UFO
SPACE
SPACE
UFO
SPACE

Want free goodies?
Email us at freebies@pbleu.com

@PapeterieBleu

@Papeterie Bleu

Shop our other books at
www.pbleu.com

Wholesale distribution through Ingram Content Group
www.ingramcontent.com/publishers/distribution/wholesale

For questions and customer service, email us at
support@pbleu.com

hi my name is...
LiLy

Bea's life

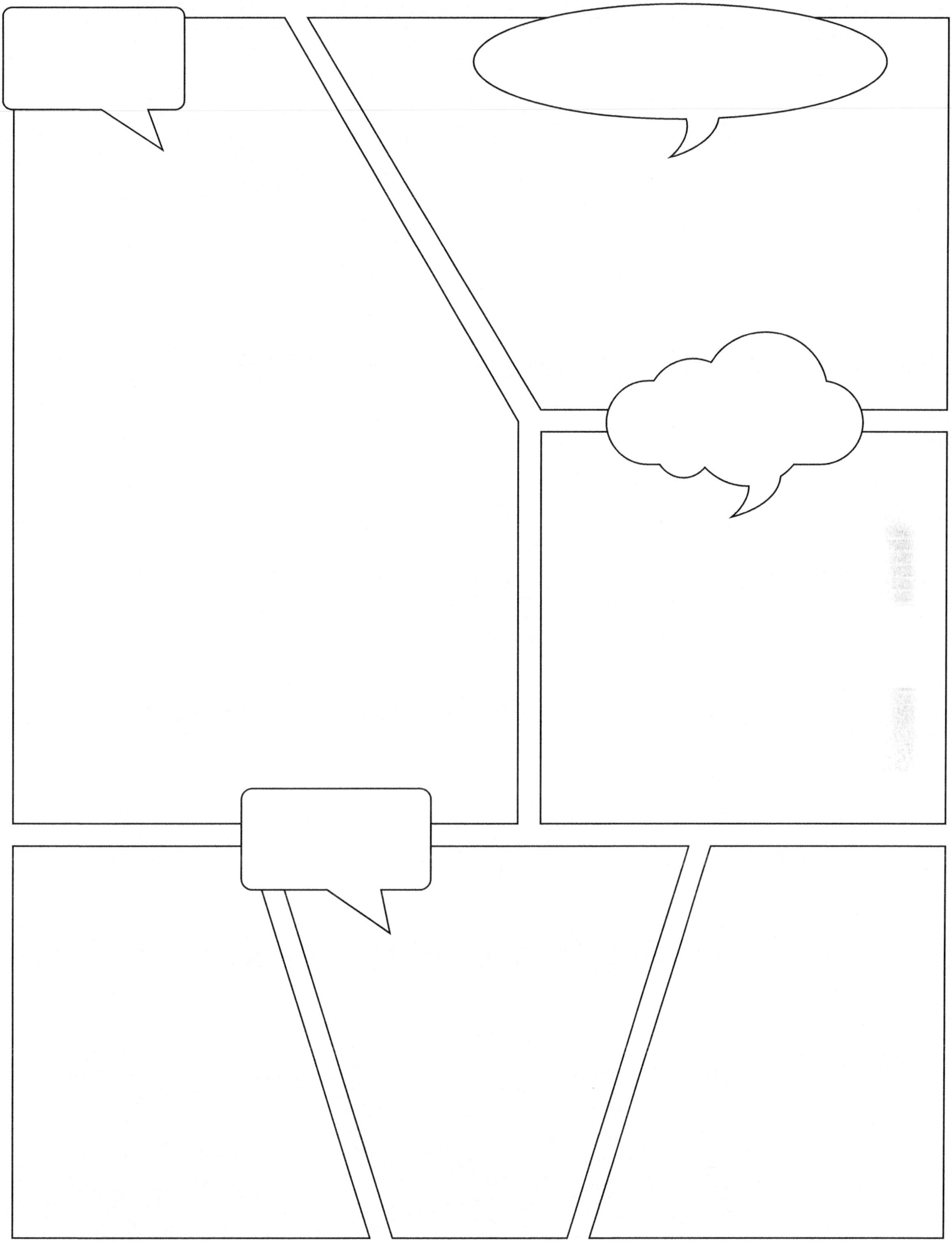

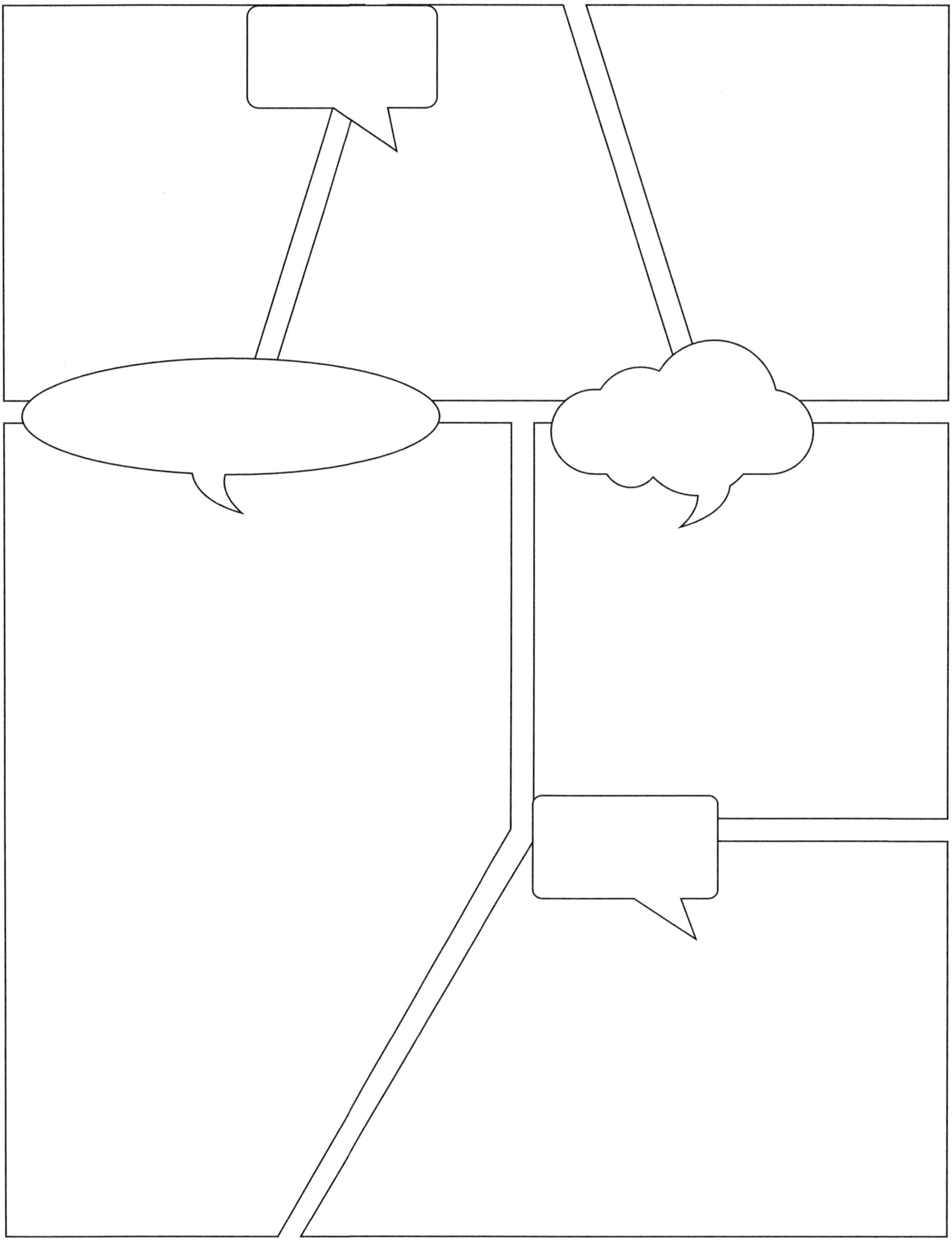

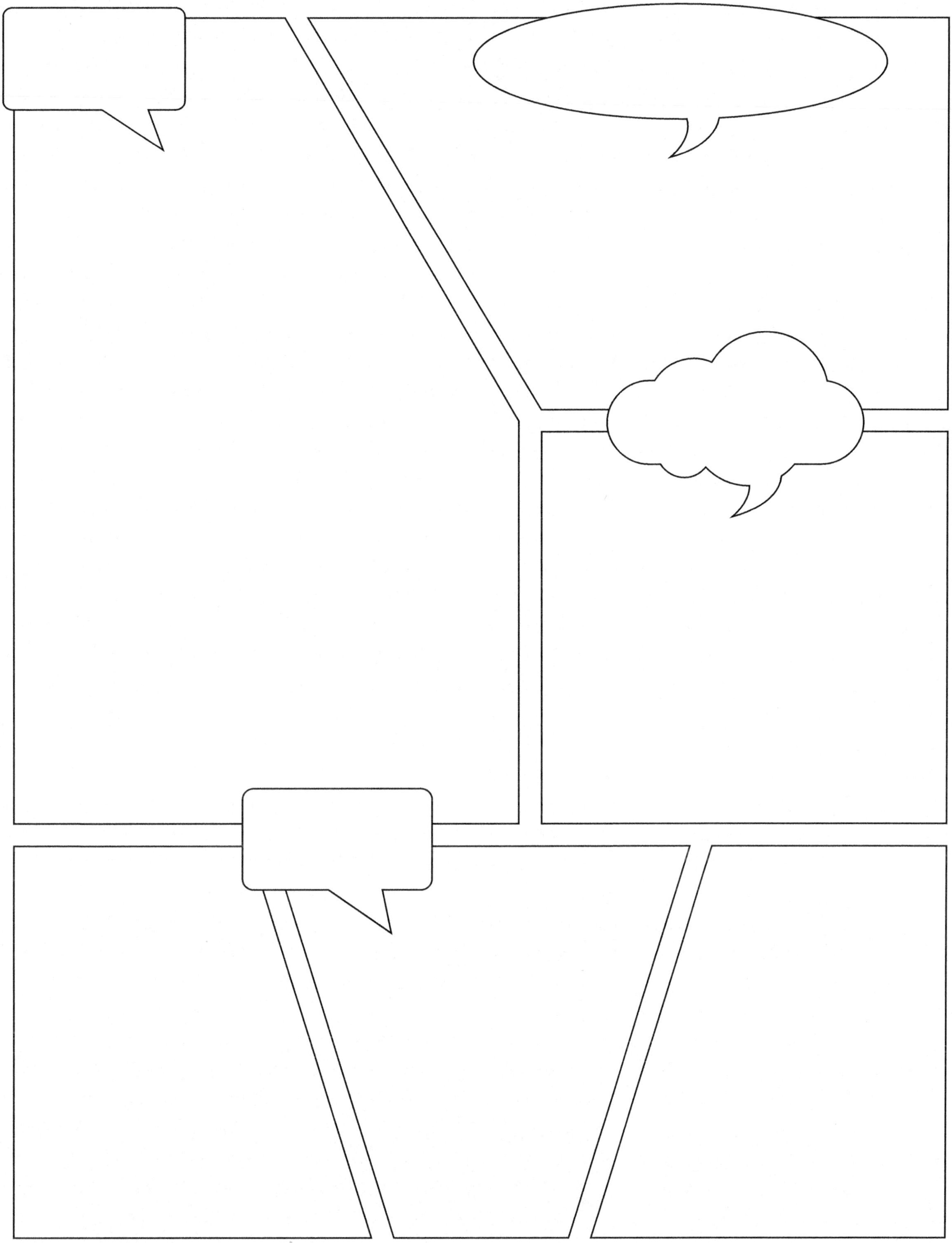

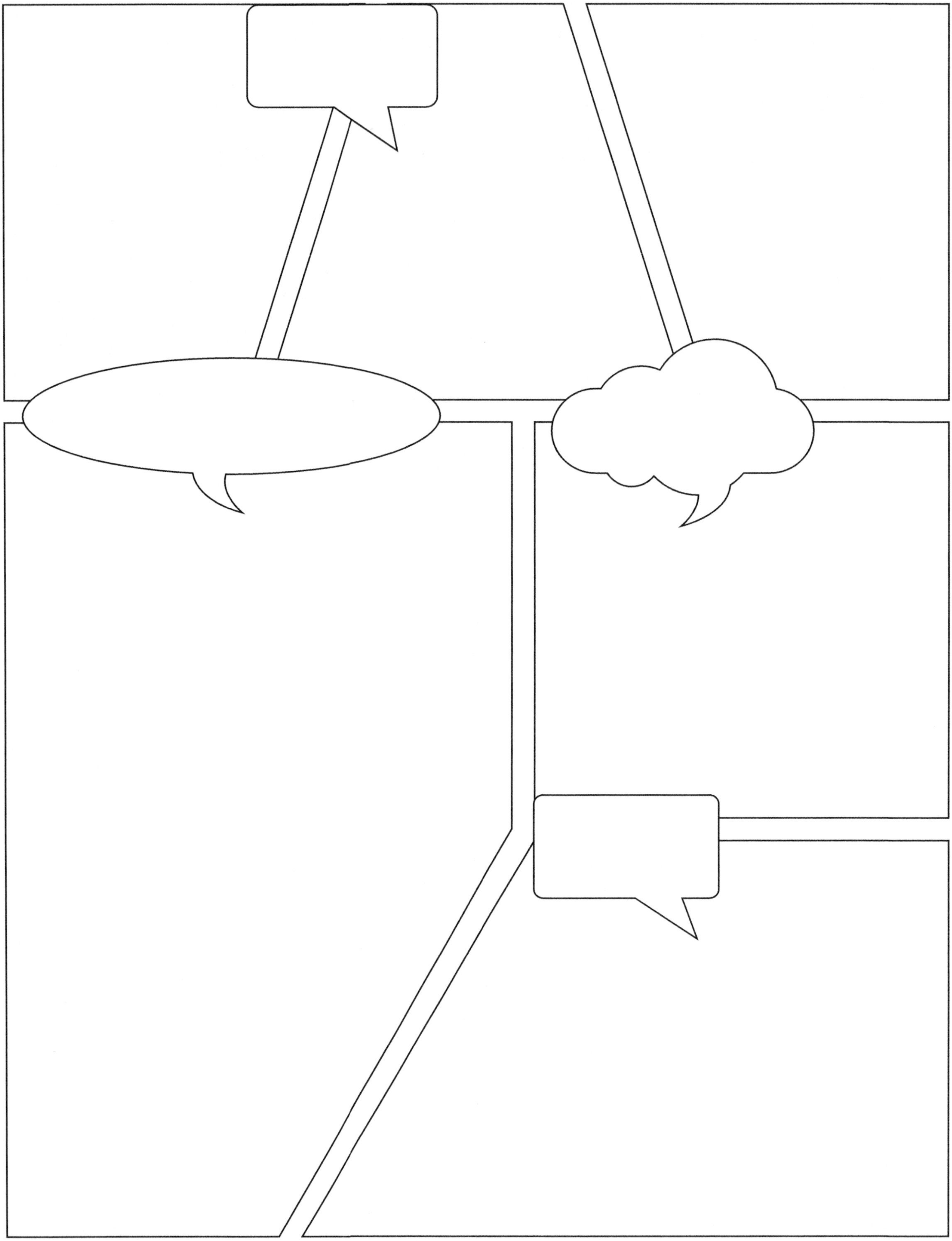

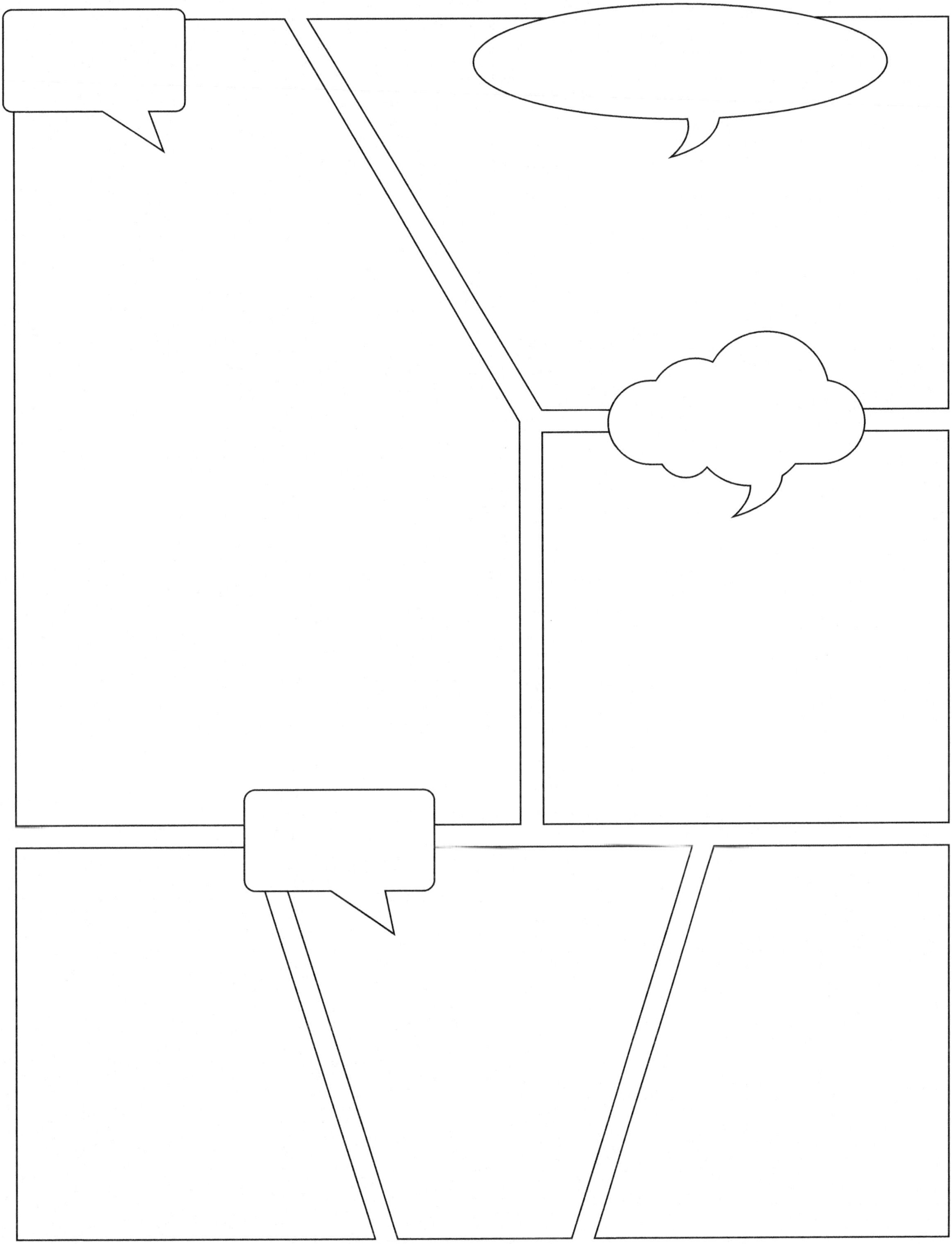

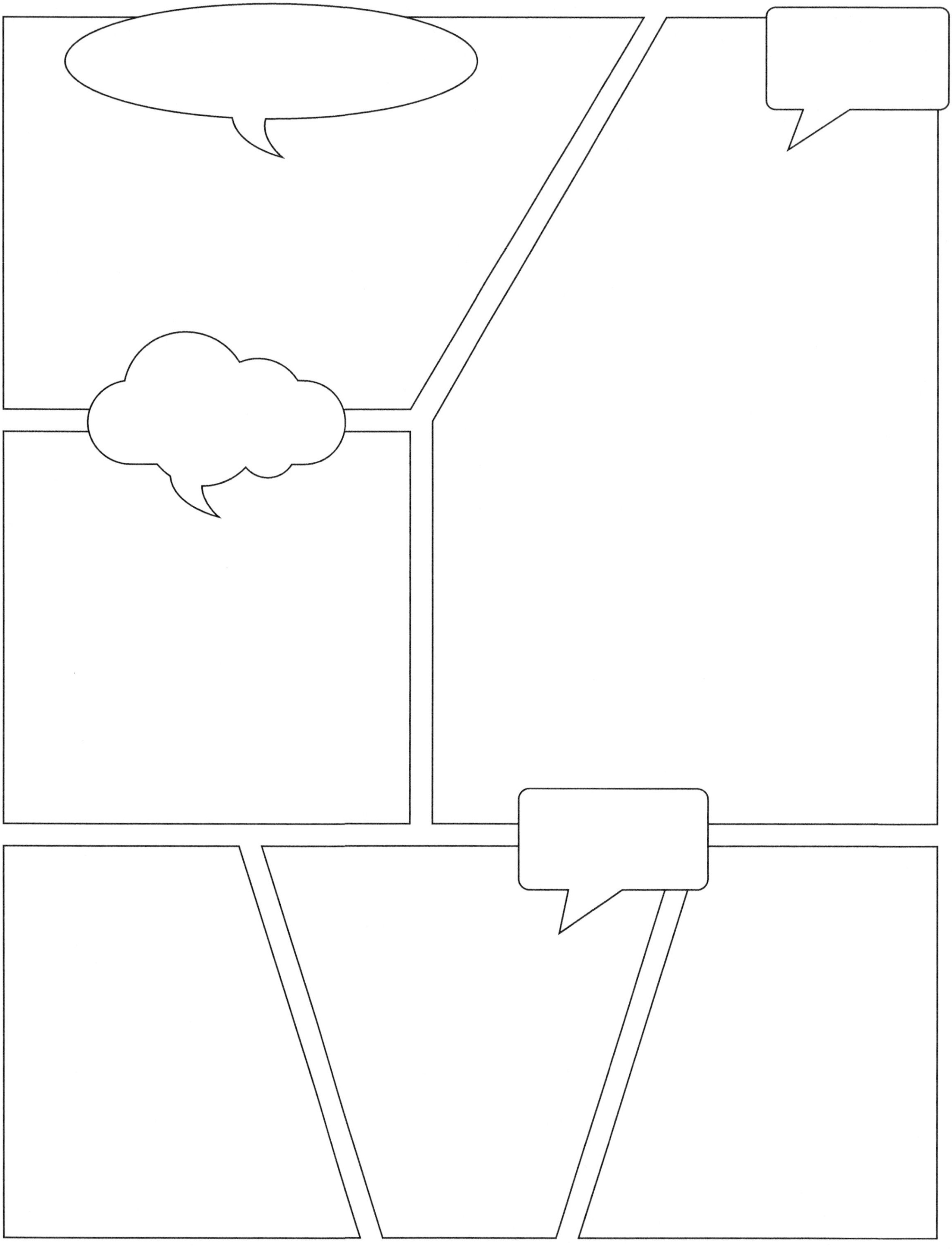

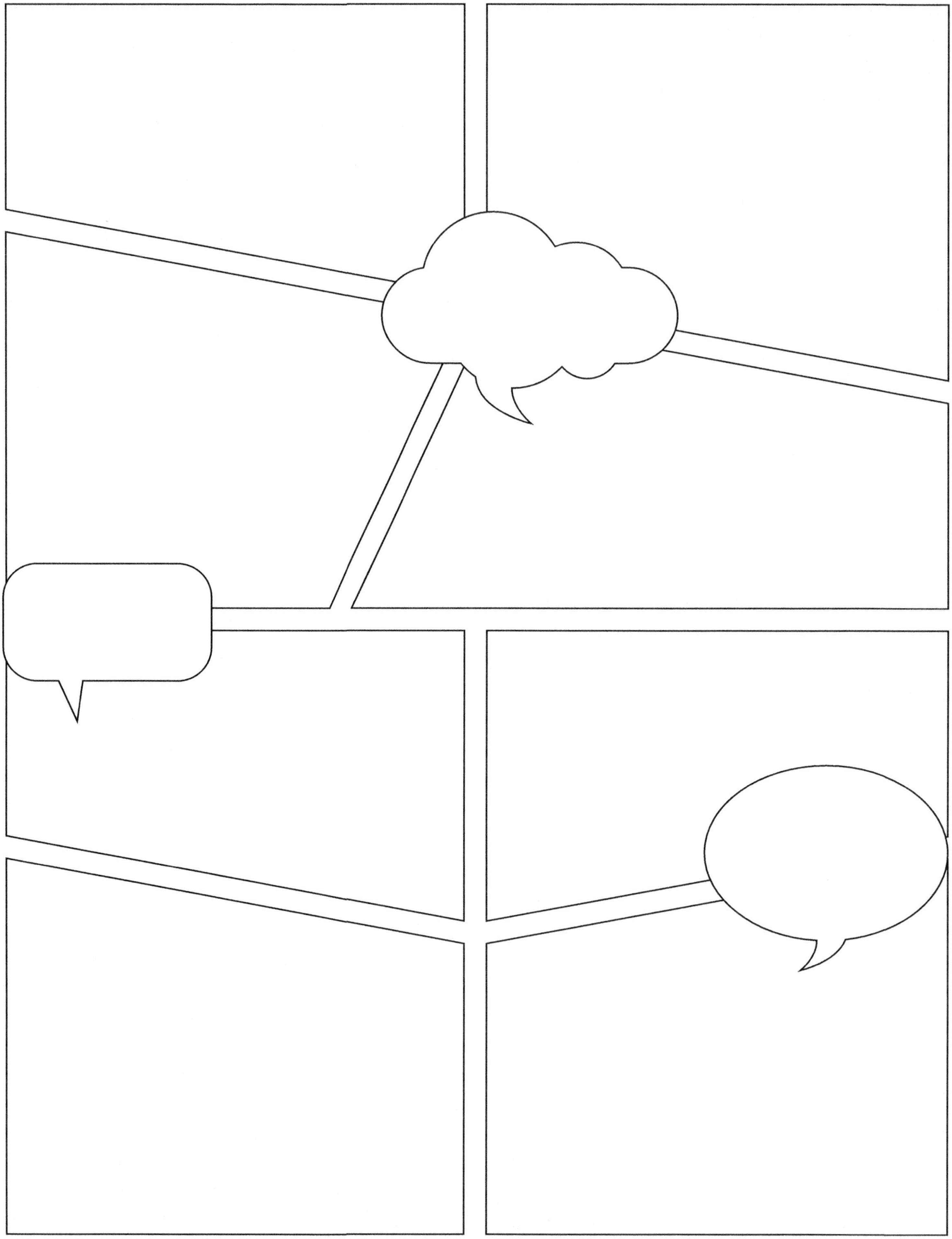

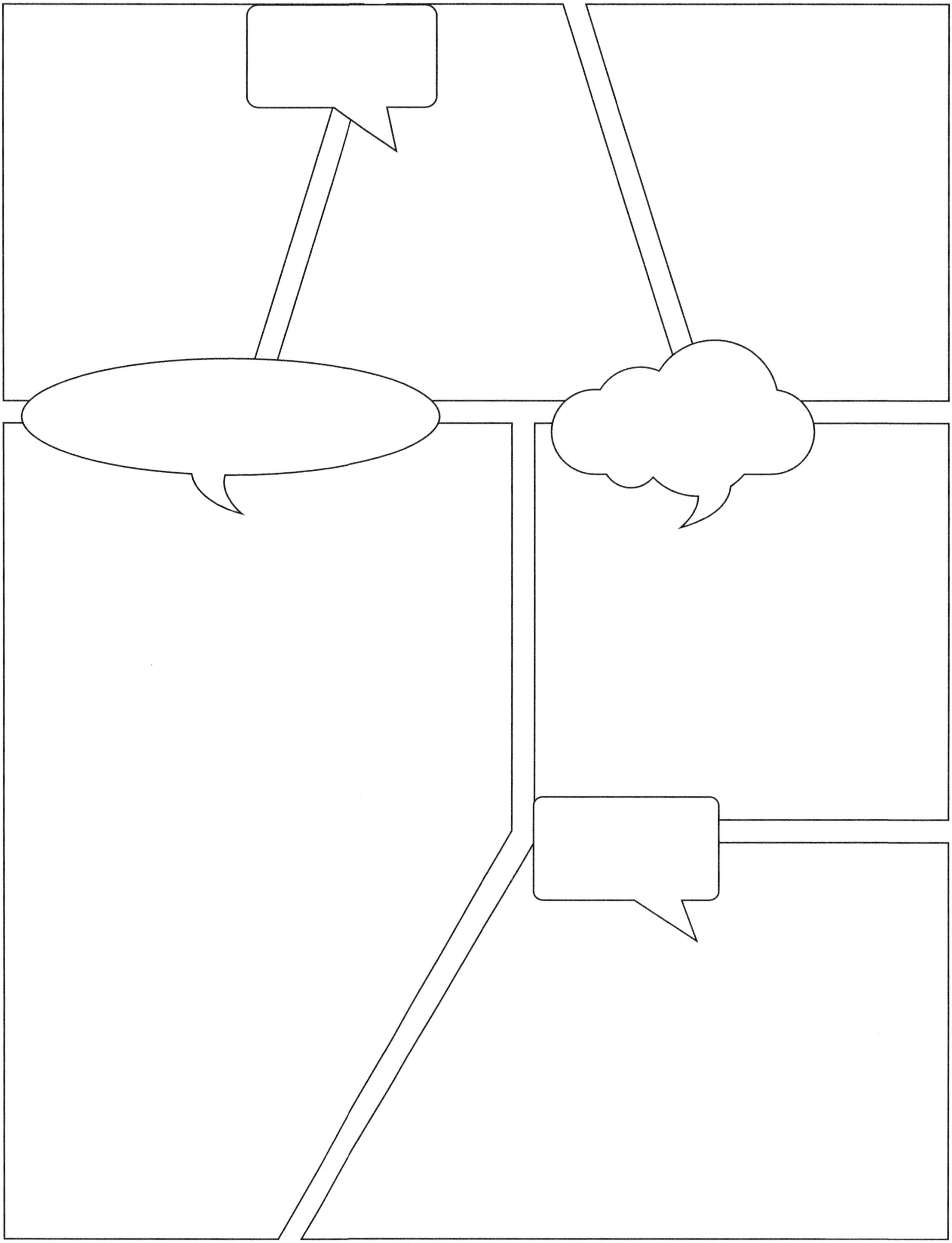

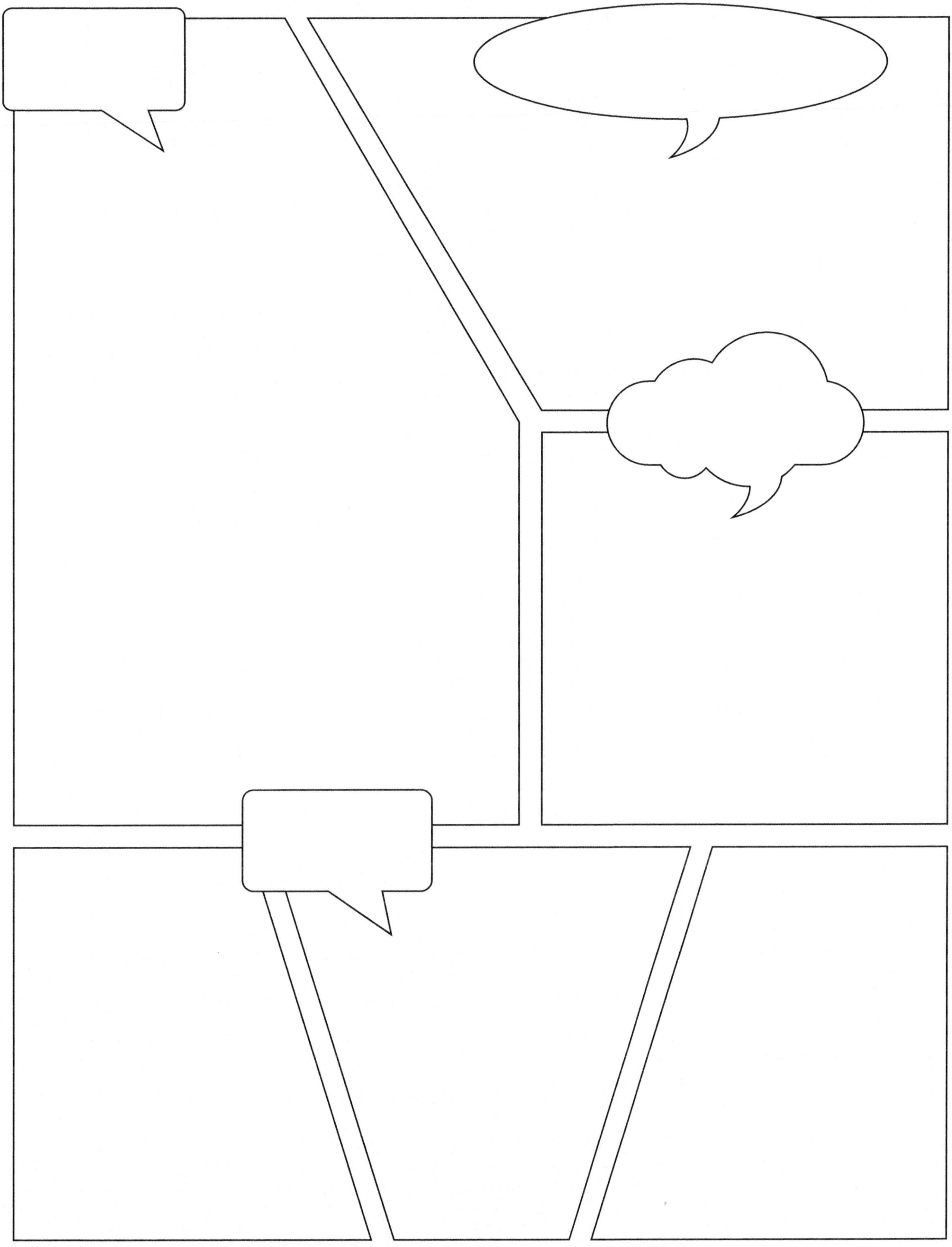

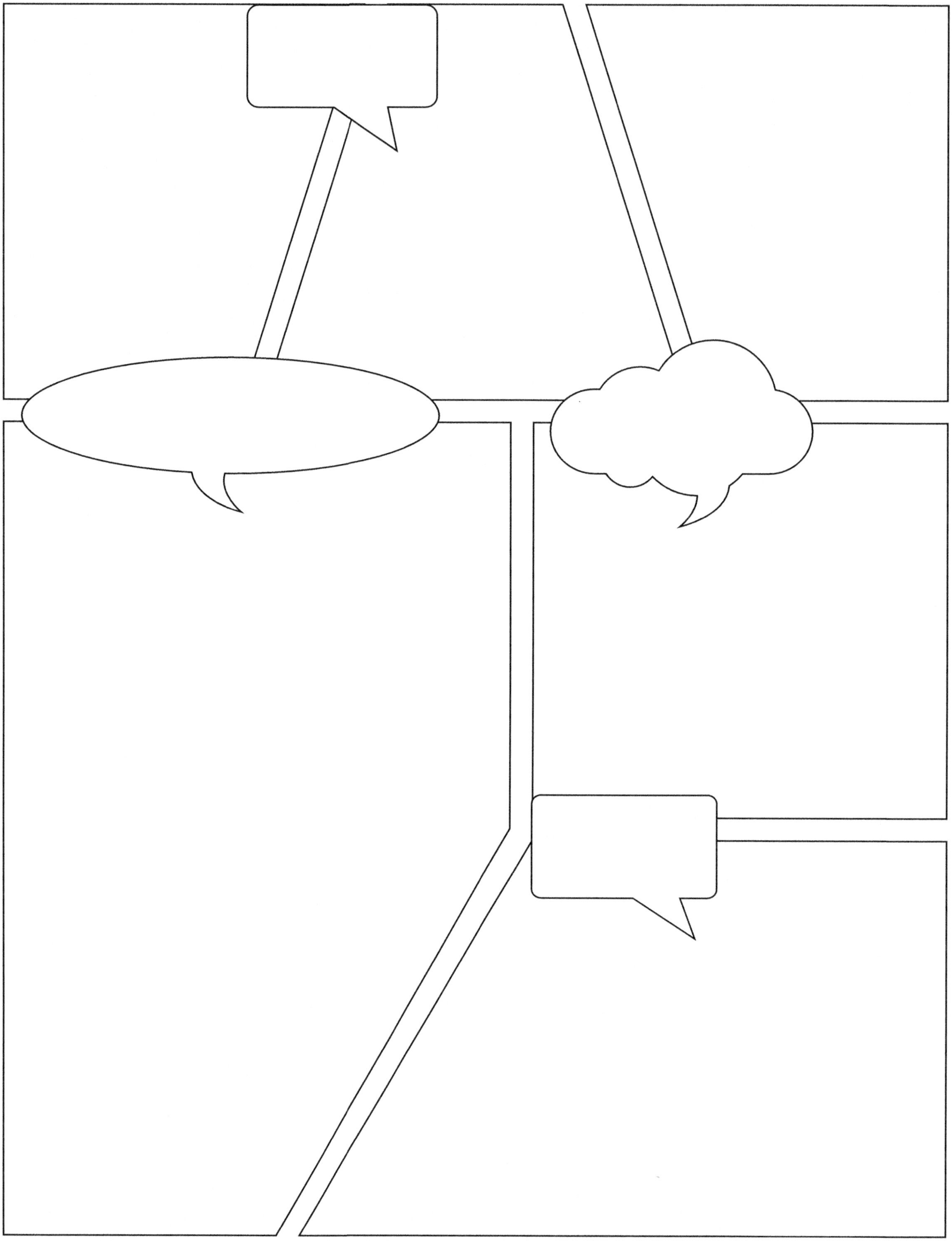

Printed in Great Britain
by Amazon

29344587R00057